WILD
SIERRA NEVADA
A FAMILY NATURE GUIDE

Joanna Howes

ILLUSTRATED BY
Alex Bailey

Yosemite Conservancy
YOSEMITE NATIONAL PARK

For Juniper, Ina, and Clayton
—J. H.

For my parents,
Caroline and Michael
—A. B.

Terms in **boldface** can be found in the glossary.

YOSEMITE
CONSERVANCY.
yosemite.org

Yosemite Conservancy inspires people to support projects and programs that preserve Yosemite and enrich the visitor experience.

Library of Congress Cataloging-in-Publication Data
Names: Howes, Joanna, author. | Bailey, Alex (Illustrator), illustrator.
Title: Wild Sierra Nevada : a family nature guide / Joanna Howes ; illustrated by Alex Bailey.
Description: 1st. | Yosemite National Park : Yosemite Conservancy, [2024] | Audience: Ages 4 to 7 | Audience: Grades K-1 | Summary: "A natural history guide for young children, presenting five categories of life in the Sierra Nevada mountains community: trees, mammals, birds, shrubs, and wildflowers. Lyrical descriptions and detailed watercolors accompany each commonly found species. A field guide for each category is included so that the the book can be taken along on outings and used to identify species"-- Provided by publisher. Identifiers: LCCN 2023007285 (print) | LCCN 2023007286 (ebook) | ISBN 9781951179298 (hardcover) | ISBN 9781951179328 (epub)
Subjects: LCSH: Yosemite National Park (Calif.)--Juvenile literature. | Natural history--California--Yosemite National Park--Juvenile literature. | Animals--California--Yosemite National Park--Identification--Juvenile literature. | Plants--California--Yosemite National Park--Identification--Juvenile literature. Classification: LCC QH105.C2 H695 2024 (print) | LCC QH105.C2 (ebook) | DDC 508.794/47--dc23/eng/20230616
LC record available at https://lccn.loc.gov/2023007285
LC ebook record available at https://lccn.loc.gov/2023007286

Design by Katie Jennings Campbell

The artwork was created using watercolors and ink on paper.
Endpapers wash by iStock.com/PJ_nice (color altered)

Printed in China

1 2 3 4 5 6 – 28 27 26 25 24

CONTENTS

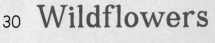

Under a bright moon on a late winter's night, the Sierra Nevada forest is still and silent. If you were to walk through it, you would see only snow glowing as if lit from within and shadowy outlines of trees. But a whole world buzzing with life exists here—and it can be a harsh place to live. Summer brings plenty of sunshine with little to no rain. Winter means months of deep snow and scarce food. The forest holds ancient stories of the ways in which every creature is perfectly suited to survive here. Explore, observe, and let the forest tell you these tales!

Trees

To figure out if the tree you found is one of the nine species listed below, first notice if it has leaves, scales, or needles.

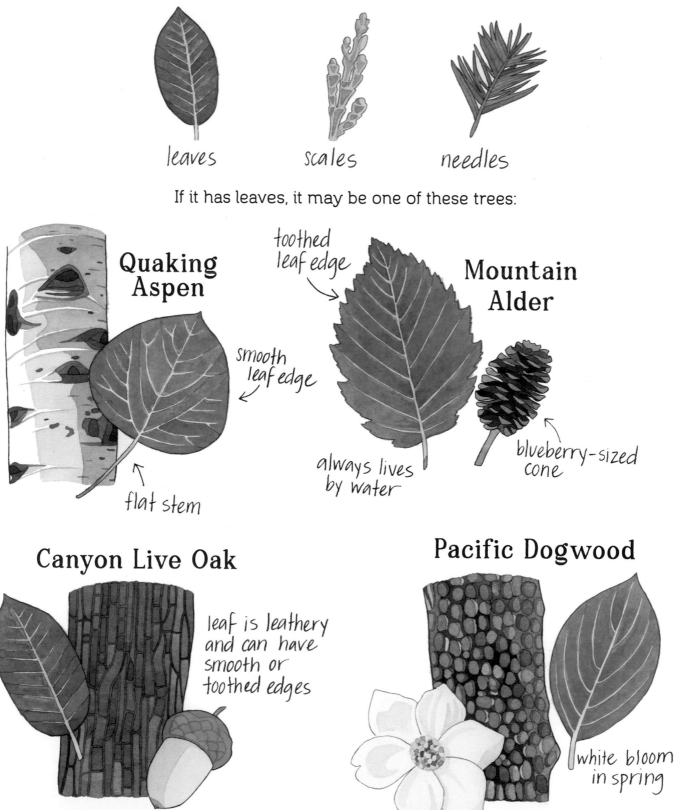

leaves   scales   needles

If it has leaves, it may be one of these trees:

Quaking Aspen

smooth leaf edge

flat stem

Mountain Alder

toothed leaf edge

blueberry-sized cone

always lives by water

Canyon Live Oak

leaf is leathery and can have smooth or toothed edges

Pacific Dogwood

white bloom in spring

If it has scales, it may be an incense cedar.

Incense
Cedar

cone shaped like
a quacking duck's bill

If it has needles, it may be one of these trees:

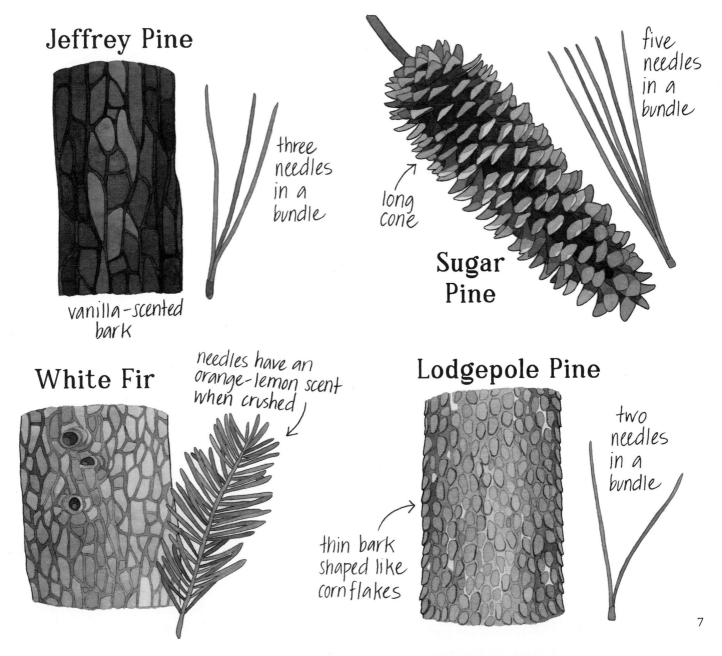

Jeffrey Pine

three
needles
in a
bundle

vanilla-scented
bark

five
needles
in a
bundle

long
cone

Sugar
Pine

White Fir

needles have an
orange-lemon scent
when crushed

Lodgepole Pine

two
needles
in a
bundle

thin bark
shaped like
cornflakes

Quaking Aspen

Most trees have round leaf stems, but aspens have flat ones that are attached in a way that makes the leaves quake with the slightest breeze. On windy summer days, the leaves twinkle like clusters of green stars, while in autumn, each golden leaf dances like a flickering flame.

Aspens are **deciduous trees**. This means they shed their leaves, which wouldn't make it through the cold of winter, so just their silvery branches remain.

Incense Cedar

Incense cedars are **evergreen trees**, which means their scaled leaves stay on throughout the winter. Their branchlets are flat; they're a little like green umbrellas. During storms, birds, bears, and coyotes may shelter under these trees.

You can often find small cones beneath the trees. If you squeeze one to open and close, it will look like a duck quacking with its tongue out.

Their thick bark may protect the trees from the fires that sweep through the Sierra Nevada.

Mountain Alder

Mountain alders have tiny cones, each the size of a blueberry. Seeds inside the cones fall out so that new trees can grow. The trees live along creeks and shorelines, and their branches often hang over water. You'd think the dropped seeds would sink, but they don't. The seeds have pockets of air in them—and because air is lighter than water, they float! The seeds are like miniature boats, each sailing to their new home.

Lodgepole Pine

While other trees' thick bark helps protect them from wildfires, lodgepoles' thin bark burns easily. These trees have a different wildfire strategy: be the first ones to grow back. They make bounties of seed-bearing cones and love the full sunshine and bare soil that fire brings.

After a wildfire, seeds drift in with the wind, bringing the hope of a new forest. If you return to a burn site years later, you may find a miniature lodgepole pine forest growing.

Jeffrey Pine

When you find these trees, sniff the resin that sits in the cracks of the bark. Some people say it smells like vanilla or baking cookies. On a breezy day, the wind sings through the trees' needles, and it sounds like

Wish, wish, wishshshshshshshshsh!

These needles also help the trees survive. During the Sierra's dry summers, their waxy cover holds in water. In winter's huge storms, the snow slips around the skinny needles. This protects the branches from breaking under the weight of heavy snow.

Jeffrey pines look very similar to another common Sierra tree, the ponderosa pine. To tell the difference, hold a cone in the palm of your hand. Does the cone prick you? If so, it is a ponderosa; if not, a Jeffrey. Just remember the phrases *prickly ponderosa* and *gentle Jeffrey*.

Canyon Live Oak

When you find canyon live oak trees, search for fallen acorns. These acorns look like they are wearing a funny hat. Called a cupule, this cap helps protect the seed inside. In the fall, acorns ripen and drop, providing a feast for many animals. Steller's jays bury them everywhere to prepare for winter. The acorns the jays forget about have a chance to become baby oak trees in the springtime.

Pacific Dogwood

In spring, the white blooms of dogwoods decorate the forest the way stars paint the night sky. In autumn, their leaves turn rosy red and remind us that winter is near.

Pacific dogwoods produce red berries that are eaten by animals. Berry-producing trees and shrubs like dogwoods are important for bears, who gobble up lots and lots of berries in late summer so they can store fat for the long winter.

Sugar Pine

Sugar pines are known for their beautiful long cones. Find one on the ground or look up at the branch tips. The pine cones are there to protect the trees' seeds hidden inside. On warm, dry days, the cones open like flowers, letting in the sun. But when it's snowing, they close up, as if tucking their seeds into bed.

The seeds have papery wings, and when released, they whir around like little airplanes, which helps them spread.

White Fir

Look up at the top of a white fir and you may see that the highest branches make a snowflake pattern against the sky.

If you crush some needles in your fingers, you may notice they smell like oranges and lemons. And, like these fruits, they are full of vitamin C.

Sometimes, a fungus hollows out the trunks of white firs, which then become cozy dens for animals. Birds make their nests there, and black bears curl up to sleep during the Sierra's cold winters.

Mammals

While there are many mammals in the Sierra Nevada forest, most remain hidden as they carry on their quiet, secret lives. The animals listed below are more easily found out in the open, and ones you're likely to see when out on a walk.

red behind ears

yip and howl at night

black tail tip

Coyote

Mule Deer

white tail with black tip

Black Bear

fur can be black, brown, blonde, or cinnamon

Here's how to tell these squirrels and chipmunks apart:

Chipmunk

stripes on its face and back

smallest of the three

Chickaree (Douglas Squirrel)

ear tufts

smaller tail than a western gray squirrel's

make a peer-o alarm call

biggest, fluffiest tail of the three

Western Gray Squirrel

NOTE: Another common Sierra animal, the golden-mantled ground squirrel, is sometimes confused with chipmunks. The golden-mantled squirrel is larger and does not have stripes on its face.

Coyote

Coyotes often sleep the day away and come out in the evening to feed on mice, rabbits, and squirrels. Known as the song dogs, they greet their family with yips and howls after a night of hunting alone. They also howl together to tell other packs "Stay away!" and bark to warn their own that danger is near. If you leave your window open in summer, you may hear the coyotes sending their eerie, beautiful song into the night.

Chipmunk

Chipmunks dig large underground **burrows**. Each burrow contains many rooms—including one covered in leaves for sleeping, one for babies, and one for food.

They carry seeds to their burrows in pockets in their cheeks. They need to store a lot of food. While their world is covered in snow, chipmunks sleep snugly underground, waking up every few days just long enough to have a little snack.

Chickaree
(Douglas Squirrel)

In autumn, look for piles of pine cone scales. These are left behind when chickarees tear apart cones to eat their seeds. They hide enough seeds from white fir and Jeffrey pine cones to get through winter. Chickarees don't **hibernate**, so you may see them out and about on quiet, snowy days.

You may notice the chickarees' alarm call, a loud, repeated *peer-o*, which often gets mistaken for a bird call.

Black Bear

It's difficult to spot the shy black bears, so we must rely on clues left behind. You may notice a pile of **scat**, a footprint in the mud, or a hollowed-out white fir just right for a den. Bears hibernate during the Sierra's cold winters, and mama bears give birth during hibernation. The cubs, born so small they would fit in your hand, stay snuggled up with their mother, drinking her milk until spring arrives.

If you do see a bear, stay calm and back away slowly. Make noise and yell "Go away, bear!" Never approach a bear. Do not allow bears access to your food—pack away all your trash!

Western Gray Squirrel

Western gray squirrels are shy tree dwellers—you won't find them in the middle of big cities. They prefer to spend their lives among the Sierra's pine, oak, and fir trees, sleeping in their trunk cavities and eating their cone seeds.

You may notice these squirrels' fluffy tails bouncing along behind them. They use their tails in many ways, such as to help balance on tree limbs and to warn off **predators**. These squirrels don't hibernate, so they may also use their tails as a warm blanket on cold winter nights and as an umbrella in storms.

Mule Deer

Mule deer are constantly on alert for predators, which include coyotes, mountain lions, and black bears. Females are especially protective of their young, called fawns, who look like they've been sprinkled with white confetti. The spots provide **camouflage**. Fawns often wait alone for hours while their mother feeds, and a predator may think they are just a patch of dappled sunlight on the forest floor.

Like many animals, mule deer **migrate** seasonally. When the first heavy snow covers the mountains, the deer retreat to the warmer Sierra foothills.

Shrubs

Shrubs are similar to trees—they have leaves and branches—but they are shorter and have many stems coming from the ground instead of just one trunk.

When you find a shrub, match the leaf to the picture—the leaves on this page are all approximately their actual size. Shrubs have flowers only certain times of the year. If you see flowers, match the flowers' color to the picture too.

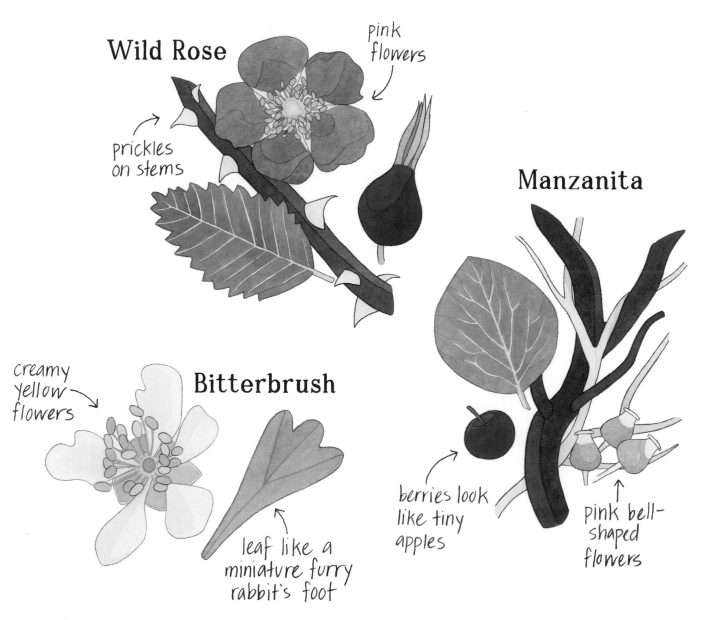

Wild Rose

pink flowers

prickles on stems

Manzanita

creamy yellow flowers

Bitterbrush

leaf like a miniature furry rabbit's foot

berries look like tiny apples

pink bell-shaped flowers

Wild Rose

Wild rose shrubs bear a winter treasure: when the forest is blanketed in snow and the berries of summer are long gone, the roses' fruits remain. Called rose hips, the fruits provide animals with nutrients they need for getting through the Sierra's long, cold winter.

You may notice the sharp prickles on these shrubs' branches. These protect the plants from being eaten by animals.

Manzanita

The manzanita's red bark twists around its dead, woody stems like a sculpture, carrying nutrients to the living parts of the plant. Rub your hand along the bark to see how smooth it is.

Peer closely at the berries—they look just like miniature apples. *Manzanita* actually means "little apple" in Spanish. Bears, birds, and coyotes all love to eat them.

Bitterbrush

Bitterbrush leaves look like miniature furry rabbits' feet. The fur on the leaves protects the plant from the sun and from losing precious water—essential for getting through Sierra summers.

These plants are named for their leaves, which taste bitter to people. But they're an important food source for Sierra Nevada animals—the leaves have many nutrients, such as protein and beta-carotene (also found in carrots). Mice and squirrels are known to farm bitterbrush: they plant seeds in the ground and then return in the spring to eat the nutritious **seedlings** that grow.

Wildflowers

Wildflowers' pretty smells and colors attract pollinators, such as insects and hummingbirds. Pollination allows plants to reproduce by making seeds to grow baby plants. Here's how it works:

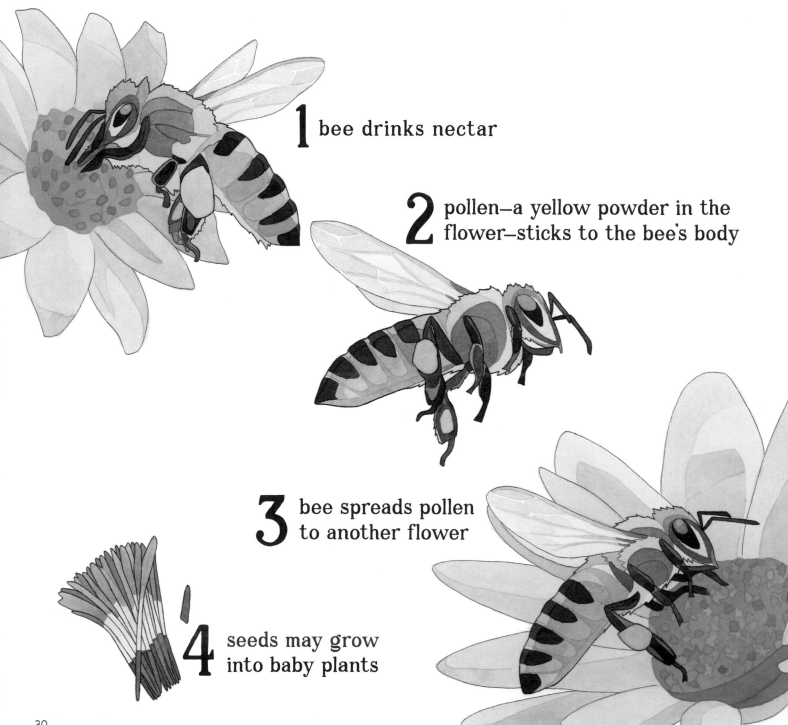

1 bee drinks nectar

2 pollen—a yellow powder in the flower—sticks to the bee's body

3 bee spreads pollen to another flower

4 seeds may grow into baby plants

To identify a wildflower, first notice the flower's color.
Then notice the shape of the leaves.

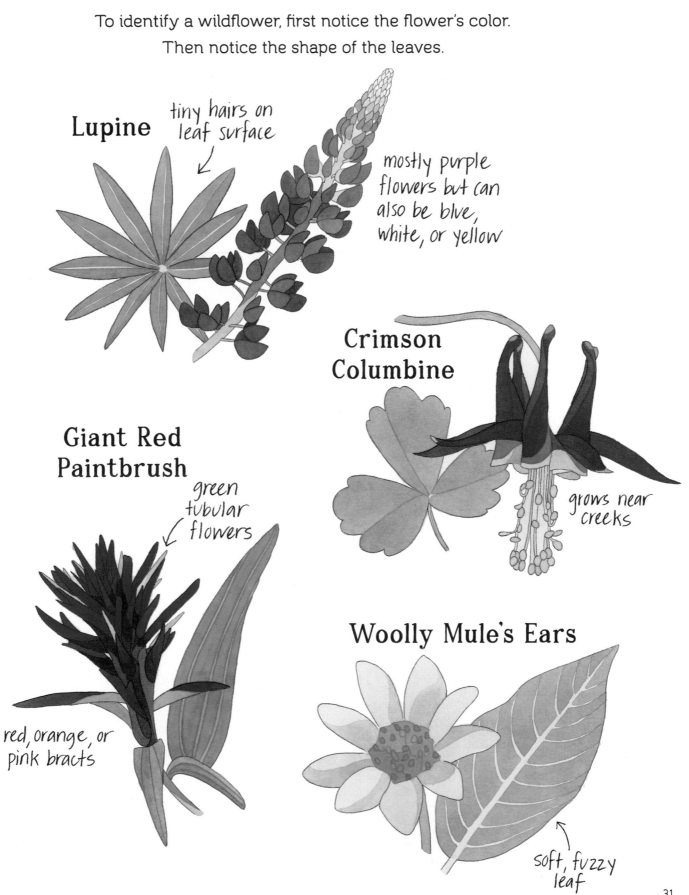

Lupine

tiny hairs on leaf surface

mostly purple flowers but can also be blue, white, or yellow

Crimson Columbine

grows near creeks

Giant Red Paintbrush

green tubular flowers

red, orange, or pink bracts

Woolly Mule's Ears

soft, fuzzy leaf

Lupine

If you see these flowers in the morning, there may be dewdrops like little diamonds in the center of the leaves. Tiny hairs on the leaves' surface help collect water, which feeds the plants.

Different kinds of pollinators have favorite colors. Though bees will visit yellow and white lupines, they prefer purple. You may notice bees buzzing all around these flowers

Lupines are also helper plants. Beneath the ground, their roots are busy improving the soil, helping other plants grow.

Giant Red Paintbrush

These flowers look like brushes dipped in bright paint—red, orange, or pink. The colored parts, called bracts, attract pollinators—but the bracts are tougher than petals, so they survive longer. The fragile green flowers are protected inside the bracts. If you look very closely, you may see them.

Like many of the Sierra's wildflowers, giant red paintbrushes are **perennials**, which means they hide underground all winter until spring wakes them up.

You may often see paintbrush and lupine flowers together. This is because paintbrush has a special survival strategy: its roots take nutrients and water from other plants, and lupine is a favorite.

Crimson Columbine

Many insects have a hard time seeing the color red, so crimson columbines are secret flowers just for hummingbirds. The flowers also have extra-sugary nectar. Hummingbirds flap their wings very quickly, so they need the sweet energy that these plants give them.

Woolly Mule's Ears

Mule's ears are a favorite of many types of butterflies that live in the Sierra. Butterflies are attracted to yellow, and the flowers' long petals make perfect landing spots. These flowers are also important for the butterflies that stop to sip nectar as they migrate through the Sierra. During their migration, you may see hundreds of butterflies glittering through the air on their tissue paper wings as they travel over mountains and through the wind on their long journey.

Birds

We hear birds more often than we see them because birds move quickly and hide really well. So the best way to get to know a bird is to watch it and listen, until you know its sounds by heart. Use the tips below to figure out which birds you're looking at, and then listen for their songs and calls. Birds sing in spring and summer, and use calls to communicate throughout the year. Most of the birds here are males. With some birds, the females look different.

black crest on its head

Call is a loud screech

Steller's Jay

White-Headed Woodpecker

usually on a tree trunk quietly flaking away bark

Northern Flicker

often feeding on ground

American
Robin

orange
breast

Red-Breasted
Nuthatch

call is
"ank ank"

usually upside down
on a tree trunk

Mountain
Chickadee

call is
"chick-a-
dee-dee"

usually hanging
upside down on
a branch

Rufous
Hummingbird

female

usually flying
by in a blur

as long as
your finger

male

red throat patch
can appear green

37

Steller's Jay

With their funny crests and loud screeches, Steller's jays seem to want to say, "I'm here, I'm here!" They can copy the sounds of animals to scare off other birds— sometimes even barking in the trees like dogs. These birds may beg for your food, but remember never to feed wildlife.

You may find their deep-blue feathers scattered around the forest floor like little gifts. However, these feathers aren't really blue—their color is just a trick of light. Hold one up against the sky and watch it turn gray.

White-Headed Woodpecker

Instead of drilling into tree trunks like most woodpeckers, these birds quietly flake away bark to find insects. But they do noisily peck holes in dead trees, called snags, to build their nests every spring.

Woodpeckers' old nest holes are then used by **cavity-nesting** birds, such as chickadees and nuthatches. When you see a snag, count how many holes you see—sometimes they're like busy apartment buildings for birds.

Northern Flicker

Flickers look like someone quickly painted them—a stroke of red on the cheeks, dots on the chest, a black half-moon like a bib.

Like all woodpeckers, flickers drum loudly on trees in the spring, to declare a place their home or to attract a mate.

Flickers are often seen on the ground spearing ants with their sticky tongues, which are so long that they wrap around the inside of their heads.

Red-Breasted Nuthatch

There's enough food for all the birds in the mountains because each species finds a meal in its own special way. Nuthatches quietly creep headfirst down tree trunks and pluck insects out from under the bark.

They can be hard to see, but if you hear sounds like invisible elves tooting horns in the forest, they're probably the nuthatches' funny ank ank call.

Mountain Chickadee

Listen—in the Sierra, you will almost always hear a chickadee. These birds can survive the winters by storing pine and fir seeds beforehand, sometimes in thousands of different places.

Their song sounds like *Cheeseburger!*—giving them the nickname "cheeseburger birds." Their call, *chick-a-dee-dee*, could be warning the other birds, "A person is near!" The scarier they think you are, the more *dees* they put at the end of their calls. How many *dees* do you hear?

Rufous Hummingbird

When rufous hummingbirds flit in the sunlight, they look like shimmering ruby and emerald jewels. Nectar from wildflowers is a main part of their diet—and because hummingbirds are too heavy to land on the flowers, they hover in place instead. Instead of flapping their wings like other birds do, hummingbirds rotate their wings in a figure-eight pattern. This allows them to hover or dart backward with a whizzing sound, like tiny bird helicopters.

American Robin

American robins love to sing! They use songs and calls for many purposes—such as giving warnings when there's danger, defending their home, or attracting a mate.

After a storm has just cleared, or in the early light of morning, it's the robins' song you'll hear floating through the trees first. And as night approaches, they chirp a very soft *tuk tuk* call from their bedtime roost, as if whispering, "Good night . . . good night!"

The Sierra Nevada is full of beauty, mystery, and wilderness. Peer closely at the flowers, smell the sweet pine air, and listen to the silvery notes of the chickadees ringing through the trees.

What will you discover?

GLOSSARY

Burrow A tunnel dug by a small animal and used as a home

Camouflage The ability of an animal to blend into its surroundings so it can't be seen

Cavity-nesting The bird behavior of making nests in dark, enclosed places, such as holes in tree trunks

Deciduous tree A tree that loses its leaves in autumn and regrows them in spring

Evergreen tree A tree that keeps its leaves all year

Hibernation The deep sleep an animal goes into for the winter to survive the cold temperatures and lack of food (verb: hibernate)

Migration The seasonal movement of animals in search of food, warmer weather, or a place to have babies (verb: migrate)

Perennial A plant whose leaves and stems die off in the winter, but because its roots remain alive, it grows again in the spring

Predator An animal that hunts and eats other animals

Scat The scientific name for animal poop

Seedling A young plant that grows from a seed

NATURAL HISTORY RESOURCES

Hansen, Keith, Edward C. Beedy, and Adam Donkin. *Hansen's Field Guide to the Birds of the Sierra Nevada*. Berkeley, CA: Heyday, 2021.

Laws, John Muir. *The Laws Field Guide to the Sierra Nevada*. Berkeley, CA: Heyday, 2007.

Storer, Tracy I., Robert L. Usinger, and David Lukas. *Sierra Nevada Natural History*, rev. ed. Berkeley: University of California Press, 2004.

calflora.org

inaturalist.org

nps.gov/seki/learn/nature/index.htm

nps.gov/yose/learn/nature/index.htm

tinsweb.org/tahome-nature-education

AUTHOR'S NOTE

The Sierra Nevada has always felt like home to me. With its soaring peaks, towering trees, and emerald waters, it is a place that sings. Whether you are a child, teacher, parent, or caregiver, I hope this book helps you deepen and celebrate your own connection with the Sierra.

One fascinating quality of mountains you may have noticed is that plant and animal communities change as you travel higher or lower. In this guide, you will find a selection of species that live at an elevation of 3,000 to 7,000 feet above sea level. For most of the species listed in this book, I use the common name, but occasionally I include only the genus. *Genus* is the name for a group of very similar species. Here, chipmunks, lupines, manzanitas, and wild roses are identified by their genus, not their many species.

I wish you joyful exploring! —J. H.

ABOUT the AUTHOR and ILLUSTRATOR

Joanna Howes has taught in Montessori primary programs for nearly a decade. She has a bachelor's degree in natural history and ecology, as well as a master's degree in education. Joanna grew up in California's Bay Area, and her fondest childhood memories include climbing granite boulders and wading in creeks on her family's annual summer trip to the Sierra Nevada. She now lives in Tahoe Vista, California, with her partner and children. Joanna loves exploring in the woods with her daughters, and you can often find her skiing, swimming in alpine lakes, and listening for birdsong.

Alex Bailey is a fine artist and scientific illustrator. She has a bachelor's degree in geology and a master's degree in environmental geochemistry. She grew up in California and spent much of her childhood visiting the Sierra Nevada. She now lives in Reno, Nevada, and draws artistic inspiration from her scientific background, her curiosity about the natural world, and her adventures hiking, rock climbing, and backcountry skiing. This is her first book. See more of Alex's watercolor artwork at alexbaileyart.com and @alexbaileyart on Instagram.